*"You see there two little figures, human beings, on the
edge of the abyss; man and woman,
two different aspects of life, two aspects of reality,
two ways of looking at reality."*
– Liane Collot d'Herbois

First published in 2023
by GlobalQuest Enterprises
PO Box 392, Maldon, Vic 3463 AUSTRALIA
www.spiritualnarratives.net
globalquest28@gmail.com

© Keith Simons 2022

This book is copyright. Apart from any fair dealing for the purposes of private study, research or review permitted under the Copyright Act 1968, no part may be stored or reprocuced by any process without prior written permission. Enquiries should be made to the publisher.

Simons, Keith, 1949-2022,
Poetica Mystica/Keith Simons.
ISBN 978-0-975836576
Simons, Keith, 1949-2022.

Cover image - Liane Collot d'Herbois fresco

Introduction

Poetica Mystica is the sequel to Poetica Estorica - an epic poem responding to Goethe's classic book *'Faust'*. Poetica Mystica especially calls forth Homunculus, the 'small human' conceieved in the laboratory, and as Rudolf Steiner tells us "Soul yet to receive a body ... Homunculus must start with what is mineral; then the realm of plants will follow ... [then] Eros unites with Homunculus: the union of the masculine aspect of the soul with the feminine aspect of the soul gives rise to the human being."(1)

In Goethe's Faust, Steiner tells us, the reason Homonculus is produced at all is so that Mephistopheles himself can become a producer of something human. "Mephistopheles is the enemy of love between the sexes on Earth. In fact, he is its archenemy. He therefore feels especially called to reduce to absurdity anything that in any way leads to love between the sexes. To rid the world of the possibility of having a human race on Earth by means of sexual reproduction is what he regards as his most important task. On the other hand, he is completely in his element in the laboratory where Homonculus is being produced. Mephistoopheles sets himself the task of producing a certain type of humanity: not one with a progressive evolution that runs its course on Earth through sexual love, but one produced along a different path. It will come from forces that have been allotted to Ahriman and will be of a very different sort than the human race that was intended for the earth."

> *"You know how we in deeply loathsome hours*
> *Planned our annihilation of the human race*
> *(Mephistopheles, in Faust) (2)*

Steiner goes on to tell us, "this science, which has grown out of this materialism, will never fully penetrate the mystery of human incarnation - never! It would [only] be able to arrive at an understanding of the origin of such beings that can form themselves in the way Homunculus does."

But the angels are here to help and intervene, and this they do. Just as each individual human being takes takes up the tasks alloted to them in Earth evolution, so too the angels go along with Earth evolution.

> *But you, who are true sons of gods*
> *Are to rejoice in Beauty, rich in life!*
> *May what's becoming, ever working, living,*
> *Embrace you with the holy bounds of Love. (Faust)*

May this poetic work contribute to the ongoing evolution of humanity and of the Earth.
—Leanne Simons, January 2023

Contents

Part One
Embodied Conscious Mystery!   7

Part Two
Deeds of Love   39

Part Three   59
Transition

Part Four
Blessings!   77

... Let us eavesdrop as a question is asked,
Inviting angelic beings to reveal, unfold,
"What ails thee?" mind asks its conjoined soul,
Why am I here and what is my goal ...

Part One

Embodied Conscious Mystery!

Through numberless streams of variegated forms,

Some unusual, others societal norms,

One impulse pulsates, generates,

Heats and cools, solidifies, evaporates,

Dwells within physical bodies,

Returns to etheric and spiritual abodes,

Tremendous variety of forms and modes,

A metamorphic spiral, gradually solidifying,

Then reversing towards far less,

Into one living cosmic consciousness,

And my friends, an evolved human bind,

Imagines itself to be separated mind,

Dwelling within an isolated body, alone,

Thinking itself into a tiny bubble,

Of flesh, nerves, organs and bone,

A bubble that in truth is a stream instead,

Stream of consciousness belonging to Godhead,

Godhead streaming, raying out,

Separating, coagulating all about,

Listen my friends, I tell you who you are,

You are conscious Godhead, infinite,

An embodied conscious brilliant star,

At once co-joined betwixt near and far,

Eternal and infinite, yet finite too,

If only your eye could intuit this view,

Co-existing in two worlds, wed this way,

Godhead's evolving, changing play,

Creator and creating, all and particular,

Manifesting as nature spectacular,

Formless and formulating, nameless and named,

Human creativity celebrated and famed,

You are all powerful, omnipotent, a miracle,

And yet limited in time and space,

Blindly groping, vulnerable, fickle,

Limited by your individuality, identity,

Unless you transcend and begin to see,

You are capable of integrating these two worlds,

Into a mystical union of wondrous beauty,

Of sacred harmony of peace alive,

That within subterranean depths you strive,

You are seeking to be all you can be,

Homo-Spiritus, Anthro-Sophia,

Embodied conscious mystery!

A caterpillar has no wings, cannot fly,

No matter how it dreams by and by,

It is earth bound with a potential secret,

A human being likewise is no angel,

Until transformed no wings as yet,

And yet has a secret of unfoldment awaiting,

Waiting a moment of mystical creating,

Here my friends, we can step beyond,

Into an ocean, out of a pond,

A tiny view, observed more grandly,

Of which a soul would become most fond,

As a process from caterpillar to butterfly,

From human to Anthro-Sophia, Homo-Spiritus,

Undergoing transition low to high,

With earthly nature providing a living metaphor,

An invisible guiding hand and more,

We can allow this metaphor to inspire,

To inform, indicate and guide,

Ignite a precious living fire,

We can ask questions that lead us well,

As revelations enter and in-dwell,

That can graphically illustrate and illuminate,

Moment by moment, no need to wait,

Mystically transforming even whilst embodied,

Such ultimately is human fate,

Many questions there are,

With unexplored responses, uncharted,

Welcomed enthusiastically once started,

Let us follow one soul on this soul journey,

Into an underworld, a cocoon containing tales untold,

Let us eavesdrop as a question is asked,

Inviting angelic beings to reveal, unfold,

"What ails thee?" mind asks its conjoined soul,

Why am I here and what is my goal,

Soul opens a portal for its guardian angel, hence,

A response because it has been summoned thus,

Inspired insights flood consciousness, whence,

Loving devotion to its human host,

Fuses together outer and innermost,

Yet in freedom's own sacred vestment,

The question repeated with more focused intent,

"What ails thee, dear soul?" reveal truly,

For I know a deep wound inhabits within,

Bringing soul into what is unruly,

So tell me the nature of this wound,

This inner torment that haunts me so cruelly,

And how to heal it, become an angel like you,

How to become Homo-Spiritus, Anthro-Sophia,

For my normal mind has not a clue,

Initiate me, then I will clearly see,

How I am an embodied conscious mystery!

Homunculus is yet forming, deforming, reforming,

Forming as all beings do through eons,

Self-created, combining elements, dawning,

As consciousness spread across the universe,

Self-aware, producing thoughts, ideas spawning,

A cosmic mystery play beyond human comprehension,

Held together with expansive, expanding tension,

Through myriads of incarnated developments,

Weaving through countless increments,

With Godhead's love of freedom intact,

Imperative original sacred pact,

Permitting free choice in nature's design,

Cosmic nature's unfolding script,

Homunculus could choose to align,

Once unified for sure, without disturbance,

Until bursting out into multiplicities abundance,

And here my friends, ways diverged,

Split asunder, realities surged,

As freedom's all-potential,

Painted on canvas's of space-time,

In unique brush strokes reverential,

Chaos belonging to life divine,

Paintings of galaxies, with shape and colour,

Uniquely their own, a moving riddle,

With consciousness occupying the middle,

Here freedom's cosmic prototype abounding,

Here the birth place of deformation,

Price paid for freedoms grounding,

Humanity reduced to state and nation,

For without falling from Grace,

Evolution would have no place,

There would be no free will,

And without deforming, no reforming,

No heart to yearn and feel,

Furthermore, without reformation,

No evolution, purpose or contrast,

Nothing creative that could last,

Homunculus, our formative soul in motion,

Reforming what has been deformed,

As an inner impulse towards devotion,

If we do now cower and flee,

Within this embodied conscious mystery!

A divergence, separation, original wound,

Homunculus was born,

History's future approval and scorn,

Propelled out of cosmic womb,

Overseeing a spectacle only it could witness,

Growth including more and less,

As Godhead's externalised eye,

Invisible yet vibrant with wonder,

Now must of necessity blunder,

Outside looking in at itself,

As an artist with astonished sight,

Forgetting much in its holy flight,

Experiencing a masterwork bedazzling.

And understanding this sublime creation,

Capable of blissful elation,

As one's own source-Creator,

Replicating Godhead as one's maker,

Hence all aligned in harmonies, beauty,

Until freedom's divine impulse begets,

Diversity with sad regrets,

Removes by dint of degree,

Cosmic mother from child,

Limits what is known as free,

And yet, is gloriously wild,

Homunculus is cut asunder,

With roars of cosmic thunder,

Umbilical cord is severed, cut,

Individuated, in relationship, but,

Forgetfulness gradually seeps in,

Daylight blinds sight from cosmic view,

This known as original sin,

Planned, therefore humanity's due,

As sun light removes starry skies,

In this way, day's myopic, blinkering,

Godhead's own creative tinkering,

Homunculus becomes a micro-identity,

This my friends, the price paid for individuation,

Separating every soul, every nation,

Original wound of separated self,

Here separation anxiety yearns secretly,

Through epochs seeking with stealth,

Edging towards knowledge of how to be,

Evolving towards an ultimate reunion,

How to merge oneself and we,

A future celebration awaiting,

Within this embodied conscious mystery!

As eons swept by, unnoticed,

Souls moved further from Spirit,

And eventually egos emerged,

Disturbing what had been merged,

Individuation had almost completed,

An outward motion, a semi-metamorphosis,

Half circle, a journey from pole to pole,

Fulfilling the circle is future's role,

Now arcing back towards its original position,

Like the waxing and waning of the moon,

But a linear extension also grew,

A faculty dangerously bold and new,

An extra ego-function, inflationary,

As mind became caught in its own web,

Sophisticated thoughts outwitted souls,

Created messy thinking, hazy goals,

Constructing a prison, cage, bubble,

Bound to lead to confusion, trouble,

Individuation became estranged,

Split, fragmented, deranged,

Overly narcissistic, manipulative, greedy,

Intellectual, lonely, anxious, needy,

And yet ingenious too in its craziness,

Believing it knows what is best,

Science and reason held at bay,

All that Spirit would have to say,

Ego-mind had won the race,

But in the process, lost mystic Grace,

Now my friends, borderland is here,

Crossroad before each human soul,

Indeed to whom the bell doth toll,

To who hears a calling, and does not flee,

From awakening within an embodied,

Conscious mystery!

Homunculus has lived through multi-forms,

Shifting sands, ever-changing norms,

We are all this archetypal soul,

As individuated entities, developing,

Incarnating, discarnating, transcarnating,

Multi-dimensional, yet joined to Godhead,

Unconsciously seeking to be Spirit led,

With an original wound of separation,

Now spread across every nation,

I, homunculus, struggle forth,

Experiencing every human desire and whim,

Until my heart and mind is full to the brim,

World weariness overtakes my soul,

Even as addictive tendencies strive,

To multiply and survive,

Consciousness witnesses it all,

Rising, consolidating and the fall,

Gradually it dawns, becomes clear,

Only one choice to be made,

Live according to Godhead's will,

Or allow all demons to invade,

Each moment, an opportunity to persuade,

To bolster or diminish,

To commit and finally finish,

To cast aside those wounded parts,

Re-transfigured in redeemed hearts,

I, you, we, can aspire, dream on,

Build foundations to live upon,

It's our collective mission to wake and see,

The march towards conscious embodied mystery!

Homunculus, evolving soul,

Carrier of a million dreams,

Where nothing is at it seems,

Torch-bearer, lover of life,

Slayer of dragons, endurer of strife,

And other demonic sprites,

That exist for their rights,

You survivor of eons,

Sleeping until awoken,

Awakening to how broken,

Every human-being becomes,

In soul nature, traversing,

Growing and reversing,

Blessing and cursing,

Homunculus, edging gradually,

Amidst ups and downs,

Suddenly ceases wandering quite lost,

Invites judgement day,

By acknowledging the cost,

Hears an angel's voice,

Stay, stay,

Fully feel the great wound,

Do not continue to stray,

Without escape or denial,

The voice continues to urge,

It's time to let go and purge,

Let this be a golden moment,

A moment secretly yearned for,

'Tis no ordinary chore,

Awaiting for will in action,

Without adversaries reaction,

To step, plunge, dive, embrace,

Choosing to about face,

Epochs of missioning, purposing,

If one could revision trace,

When homunculus emerges to be,

Inducted into conscious embodied mystery!

An emergence into a golden moment,

Deepened, expanded, melted into,

Accepted through and through,

Entire cosmos swallows,

Entire self embraces,

Homunculus obediently follows,

Receives sweetest graces,

Furthest meets nearest,

Homunculus scans surroundings,

All now appears dearest,

Everything small like a paint stroke,

That will chose to invoke,

On a massive miraculous canvas,

Where wildflower and distant star,

So close and yet so far,

Intimately related sublimely,

As consciousness sways divinely,

A concertina, music made in movements,

In and out, rhythmically dancing,

Evolution's plan mystically advancing,

A sunflower opening its yellow face,

To Father Sun in bright embrace,

Reaching a point in cosmic space,

When balance seeks to re-trace,

Closing in on itself, turns inward,

In obedience to Mother Moon,

A celestial mystical boon,

In this manner, Homunculus traverses,

Understands advances and reverses,

Between all realms, great and small,

Turn about when you hear the call,

All becomes a golden moment,

Within which questions loom,

Further guidance to transform the gloom,

Hovering insistently demanding attention,

When will my wound be healed forever,

Or is there only a truth named never,

When will my soul enter paradise,

When will my destiny be sealed,

Can such wisdom be revealed,

Questions that sublimely entice,

When will a golden moment,

Be met with eternal advice,

As timeless peace and conscious joy,

What knowledge must homunculus employ,

What wounded demons must fade and slip,

Must surrender their ruler ship,

Homunculus has reached a threshold,

So near seems this living gold,

Then peers into a magnificent and terrifying abyss,

Suddenly nothing is perceived as amiss,

Witnesses in a flash of enlightened sight,

A lucid translucent infinite light,

Beckoning, inviting, patiently waiting,

Boundless Godhead's glee,

As conscious embodied mystery!

Think of a grand tree, regal, tall
Untouched by anything impure,
Only answering to nature's call,
And yet in time foreign outgrowths occur,
What was clear now a blur,
Parasitical additions, also beatific wonder,
Merging, both having a life of their own,
Freedom's imperative no random blunder,
What is reaped has been sown,
Becoming a part of our tree's existence,
My friends, think of this metaphoric tree,
How it mirrors human striving to be free,
Layered realities, interspersing, admixing,

That now an original prototype existing,

Is shrouded in hybrid's matrix grip,

Both delightful and horrendous,

Challenging soul to choose and strip,

Environmental add ons, permitted by freedom,

Permitted by Godhead's cosmic lore,

Unpredictability is freedom's store,

A tree un-fettered by strict constraints,

Having to endure endless complaints,

Able to grow in unpredictable orientations,

For tree, cosmos and human,

Instruments for Godhead's manifestations,

Imbued with sacred artistry abounding,

When souls align with Spirit astounding,

A tree thus symbolises the human condition,

Poetically meaningful rendition,

A metaphor bespeaking of evolutional potential,

Transformation deemed most essential,

Directly encouraging you, dear soul,

Your indigenous soul nature, intact and whole,

That has been adulterated, contaminated,

Free will experimenting yet indoctrinated,

But adornments bless as well as curse,

Some hybrid additions complement,

Otherwise useless would be such verse,

A mere indulgence and way to vent,

Rather choices can be Spirit infused,

Souls can be inspired, intent,

Even glorious, beautiful, grace-filled outpourings,

Explicate harmony from inner moorings,

My friends, discernment is yours to choose,

What tree variation you can create,

You have nothing real to lose,

Nothing to deflate or inflate,

What symphony you can compose,

Homunculus standing at cliff's edge,

Daring to let go of a stagnant ledge,

Daring to leap into a golden future,

To truly know how to be free,

As conscious embodied mystery!

Part Two

Deeds of Love

...For light and dark belong together,
Sol and Luna a couple wed,
Two birds of a greater feather,
When all is done and all is said ...

Homunculus looked into her eyes,

Witnessing cosmic intelligence,

With sensitive numinous sense,

With single holy eye open wide,

Beauty manifested, Spirit fleshly endowed,

Her movements gracefully astride,

And he intentionally vowed,

To see into her soul, and proclaim,

I'll never be the same again,

Truly multi-dimensional, translucent,

Incandescent, heaven sent,

But how can eye's narrowed view,

Dulled and seeing superficially,

Saddened heart sinking too,

Floating on the surface of perception,

Can become open reception,

Seeing angels beneath human disguise,

Beyond cleverness, clear and wise,

How, blinded eyes to see clear,

How, enslavement to become free of fear,

When beloved's presence endeared,

Can remain spirit steered,

Ask Homunculus, sincere and true,

Receive a hint, indication, clue,

For one soul's journey has commonalities,

Common threads beneath banalities,

Not that Homunculus has truly won,

A battle in truth barely begun,

And yet, in this complex epic tale,

Once great single eye awakened,

New pathways replace what is stale,

Dying ghosts sacrificed, forsakened,

Spectres leaving, they will flee,

Love finally will set you free!

Homunculus now takes on other names,

Complexity takes over, it now reigns,

Humankind has become quite modern,

Welcome to transforming brains,

Souls reaching concrete forms of self,

With layers of additional strains,

A future insertion for better health,

Substantially matched by language broad,

Yet shadows follow when souls are called,

Growth without dangers cannot be,

Do not give in to being fooled,

Homunculus is a second self, an ego,

Universal cosmic self, Godhead,

Creating external mirror image to show,

Reflections so as to truly know,

That soul and ego are Spirit led,

Homo-Spiritus being when they are wed,

Human being wed to human becoming,

Like guitar and hand together strumming.

My friends, meditate on observer alone,

Until you transcend and feel at home,

Homunculus has now a chosen name,

Initiated into an evolving social game,

Language itself takes on a life of its own,

Casting its shadow power, a wind blown,

Strengthened by a storm of autonomy,

Perpetrating a divisive duplicity,

Confounding God-Self as a magician's spell,

Mind behaving most unwell,

Temptations now thriving until,

Dissatisfaction cripples the will,

A moment arrives when Self resurfaces,

When homunculus has had its fill,

When a startling insight enters the scene,

Love transforms as has always been!

Homunculus is who you think you are,

But in truth it is a creature invented,

Like soft clay with images indented,

At worst as Frankenstein let loose against,

His creator as a madman demented,

Here a replication of cosmic adventure,

Godhead's creature out of control,

Acting without discipline or censure,

The servant behaving as master of all,

Every agony, anxiety and confusion,

Compounded by habitual illusion,

And yet my friends, Homunculus is better than,

A nightmare that apposes Godhead's plan,

Look at the universe and earthly nature both,

Where is random chaos to be seen,

Spirit eye will observe an oath,

That holds all in balance despite a screen,

A facade that blinds, grips souls in a vice,

Even suggests God's playing dice,

And when homunculus finally begins to awake,

A chorus is heard, for heaven's sake,

Angels rejoice for they are our kin,

Every time a human does truly begin,

They urge for an insight to become acts of will,

Choosing actions that thrive and lovingly fulfil!

Homunculus has suffered greatly in his way,

History tells this story partly,

Incrementally inching towards judgement day,

Honest confession that won't go away,

In admission of a wound felt so deeply,

And how one's soul has avoided often,

Through countless embodiments,

Has attempted pain to soften,

Untransformed suffering distorting intents,

Ah, homunculus has suffered so,

Such a tale of endured woe,

But my friends, now a turn about,

No other ruse will win the day,

No other artifice can let him out,

Of a many walled prison cell,

Of a wounded escapist hell,

And now he stands within energy pain,

Mustering forces that can only gain,

Release and alchemical redemption,

Homunculus will never be the same again,

All therapeutic practices aimed at this,

Only path to living bliss,

Whether spiritual, mystical or secular bound,

Encountering the wound fully, it is found,

Is the portal into a healed domain,

Regardless how known by fame or name,

In past eons desires to escape were massive,

Running fast or inertly passive,

Now finally surrendering to feeling the wound,

Not easy but a promise of how to live,

And as through a window flies a dove,

Suddenly an invitation to heal in love!

Understand then my dear friends,

How homunculus was made and why,

That when soul nature descends,

It links earth with sky,

When soul incarnates into a human body,

Lowest disconnects from most high,

Because in this manner it furthers well,

To enhance a sacred pact, a holy spell,

That a second self through language made,

Godhead chose and so did bade,

The way the cosmos should be played,

Across eons into human speech,

Extending evolution's reach,

Homunculus embodied thus in flesh,

With intellect casting imaginations mesh,

A miraculous adjunct to nature's lot,

Godhead's created polyglot,

Now through thought and speech alone,

Individuated world views all one's own,

Godhead had mouths to devise,

Perspectives foolish or most wise,

Homunculus lives as Godhead's voice,

To express in freedom in selective choice,

This my friends is why it's so,

Why Creator's intended hidden show,

Has led to language in many tongues,

That between us we can bestow,

Reflected wisdom from above,

And above all else, divinely inspired love!

Striving behind a screen external,

Homunculus yearns to be reborn,

Deep down longs for the eternal,

Eventually hears the sacred call,

An emerging voice internal,

No longer denied at all,

Now a struggle ensues,

Between forces most disparate,

Quite different thoughts and views,

Incoherent shades and hues,

Microcosm inherently imbued,

With sleeping head in familiar guise,

And awakening self becoming wise,

This my friends an archetypal threshold,

Homunculus realising mind as instrument,

Gifted as Godhead's need to enfold,

Evolving into living conscious gold,

When raging battles within and out,

Subdued, transformed, without a doubt,

Homunculus knows this battle well,

Once having visited illusion's hell,

Knows how old habits die hard,

Often choosing to remain in a prison cell,

Knows inner anguish as desires prevail,

How frustrated outcomes must entail,

Held under a demonic spell,

An inner war of tormented soul,

Fragmented, frustrated, instead of whole,

And yet this is a mere postponement,

Not what is truly meant,

Homunculus yearns for blissful life,

Beyond a circus full of strife,

Confesses this tale of woe and sadness,

A stricken epic in grief so rife,

Musters increased resolve to overcome,

Mephisto's monotonous thudding drum,

Feels remorse for wasted hours,

That reduced soul life, made it dumb,

Now, opens a window, lets fly in,

A dove of peace on the wing,

Begins to honour soul's true identity,

Re-shaping thought in affinity,

A beautifully fitted hand in a glove,

A reward of becoming embodied love!

Back and forth our epic moves,

Into unknown lands and familiar grooves,

Flies high to vistas beyond the senses,

Sinks low to graveyards confined by fences,

From daytime consciousness in clear outline,

To night's mysterious play divine,

Dimensions traversed, intertwined,

Homunculus often these worlds has mined,

Glimpsing truths so grand, inspiring,

That cosmic appetites are desiring,

To inculcate, imbibe, absorb, become,

As the sun during morning rising,

And from perspective born of wonder,

Shadows sacrificed happily,

Soul and spirit bound to be,

Spreads its winged thoughts clear and free,

Often within darkness paradoxically,

For light and dark belong together,

Sol and Luna a couple wed,

Two birds of a greater feather,

When all is done and all is said,

In this manner Homunculus strives,

To integrate night and day,

A movement across dimensions,

In this awesome mystery play,

Gradually soul evolving near,

Homo-spiritus, Anthro-sophia,

Future Self both human and holy,

Beckoning Homunculus to be,

To bring sacred vision of inherent potential,

Cosmic imprint pulsing, essential,

Into golden moments of life transfigured,

Woven incredibly like strings of pearls,

Transforming time itself into mystic whirls,

An altogether sanctified mode,

Godhead's intended loving abode!

Part Three

Transition

This the ebb and flow of love,
What dearly comes must also go,
Without pain of loss, love wouldn't blossom,
And beloved art wouldn't show ...

Homunculus has suffered greatly indeed,

A natural consequence of freedom's course,

Instigated as a cosmic seed,

Godhead's hidden evolutional force,

For with freedom divergences must occur,

Consequences Homunculus must incur,

Gradually leading to a point,

When wilfulness with extra spur,

Will invite spirit to anoint,

Soul and will then must concur,

Make no mistake my dear friends,

Ti's an act of will that breaks the chain,

Allowing soul to regain,

It's birthright as seeded by,

Godhead's all seeing eye,

That eventually a moment met,

When Homunculus can learn to fly,

Released from physical identity,

Spiritual perception then to be,

A multi-dimensionality,

At ease in all worlds in harmony,

This is hope beyond illusion,

An ever present possibility,

A small step out of confusion,

Surrendering to a mystic fusion!

Along this winding story line,

Traumas varied, yours and mine,

Could not be any other way,

If freedom was to be a part of the play,

And hence, through countless births and deaths,

Everything collapsed, disintegrated,

Stripped away, transfigured, deflated,

Every attachment severed, removed,

Except one seed invigorated,

That seed ever initiated,

Rebirth secretly ever fated,

And my dear friends, soul has waited,

Percolating in subterranean depths,

'Tis for this we have been created,

For renewal must follow certainty,

In spirit realms, inner knowing validated,

Do not grieve too many days,

As greater deeds will be incorporated,

Finer, glorious, beatific ways,

Inspirational, magical forms instigated,

Mark my words, a lion will transform,

For no soul can cling to a forever norm,

Once a lion, fierce and proud,

Now in transition, not as loud,

Ahead be it known, a wolf,

A loyal leader of the pack,

Wolf-man on another adventurous track,

So it is as a Lion-hearted soul moves,

Towards other fascinating grooves,

Integrating gifts most sublime,

That will once again truly shine,

In whatever guise it manifests,

Whatever striving and artistic quests,

Was flamboyant to a tee,

Expression original and free,

But now meandering transition,

Towards another spirit led mission,

Now, celebration of a life well lived,

A glorious hallelujah sung rendition,

Farewell lion-hearted until we meet,

In reunions sumptuous and sweet!

Burning fires of loss remain,

When loving connection cut again,

Yet I tell you strong and true,

Whoever's loved comes back to you,

This the ebb and flow of love,

What dearly comes must also go,

Without pain of loss, love wouldn't blossom,

And beloved art wouldn't show,

Homunculus bursts vale of tears asunder,

Beyond the bubble he does grow,

Transforming stagnant layered rubble,

Into Spirit regions does he flow,

His insights beckon tears indeed,

As grasping is released and freed,

Mortality is seen as clothing,

Covering a soul that is roving,

Passing through external scenes,

Temporary vistas, unfolding,

He enters into a greater realm,

Into timelessness, ever present,

With contentment at the helm,

Simply alive, aware, existent,

Homunculus is transitioning,

A profound reborn positioning,

Eternity and time melding,

And super-consciousness listening!

A moment unlike any other,

Entirely of your free choosing,

Mystic eye opens wide,

Freedom without aimless cruising,

Spiritus with human astride,

Homunculus tethered wisely,

This a treasure not easily won,

As many habits must be undone,

Yet ultimately moments of pure intent,

Winged gifts heaven sent,

Invited by supernal act of will,

Beyond what homunculus can invent,

Homo-Spiritus, in Godhead's image,

Holy Sophia, a sacrament,

All in all, spherical dynamic union,

A cosmic dance of many moves,

With a choreographer's single eye,

A harmony that heals and soothes,

That weds low and high,

Here a sacrifice of fondest love,

Descending Grace from above,

Here a moment of divine supreme,

Greater than any Homunculan dream,

Chosen by soul in spiritual mind,

Beyond every lesser double bind,

This a destiny moment of vast import,

Homunculus no longer lost and blind,

The promised land, a star shining bright,

Within each soul its eternal light!

Homunculus hears these words,

Within yet a glassy enclosure thick,

Words enhancing anxiety, disturbs,

Making him feel queasy, sick,

Knowing he must eventually pick,

Choose a destiny pathway sincere,

With consequences dire and great,

Influencing ways to direct and veer,

Freedom's part in sculpting fate,

He was granted free will to play,

In sensual physicality, so to sate,

His human appetites in that way,

Addictive longings kept him prey,

Mephisto a parasite living through,

Homunculus as host in mammon's realm,

Eden's gardener became a slave,

He receives these words as a wave,

And wonders who is at the helm,

Then in a startling flash of altered mood,

Sitting in peace and solitude,

He vows a solemn wish, with heart,

To make a finer brand new start!

How many monkeys were on his back,

Carrying around monkeys in a sack,

For countless, agonising years,

Suppressed un-cried tears,

Homunculus, a self created other,

An imaginary sister or brother,

Now a vow to bring him in,

To merge with his spirit twin,

Together they can meet the day,

Forge a sacred loving way,

In a manner, a death indeed,

Of Mephisto's destructive creed,

Those monkeys no longer weighty,

Soul has been finally freed,

They have been transformed,

Into humble servants, reformed,

And in the silent heart of this,

A naturally arising wave of bliss,

The key that unlocked this mighty door,

Crystalline consciousness does implore,

Wilful compassionate intent, for sure,

Then all monkeys will devote themselves,

Become as Hanuman in mythic pose,

A consequence of intent well chose,

Sacred homeostasis, supreme balance,

Authentic intelligence has arose!

Each time you fall, pick something up,

It has been told by a wise soul,

Don't stay immobile in a hole,

Homunculus has fallen many a time,

Has payed a price, a heavy toll,

But he is learning gradually,

To remove blinkers so as to see,

For prose a plenty has he heard,

Promising of a judgement day,

When he can fly free as a bird,

And only loving wisdom will he say,

He has seen the promised land,

Often has sipped ambrosia,

Glimpses of what can be his own,

Awakening from amnesia,

A fountain spreading across the globe,

Reaping what has been sown,

He knows beyond a shadow of doubt,

That 'tis the way wind can be blown,

Only now to embolden his will,

To invite what is worthwhile to feel,

When falling into familiar pits,

To clearly learn what must heal,

Take heart my friends, journey of,

A thousand miles, will surly reveal,

Better moves made with inspired zeal,

Do not despair in view of weakness,

Opportunities beckon endlessly,

Do not give up in daunting stress,

An opening presents for you to see,

A moment of acceptance in humility,

Pick up a nugget from down below,

Hold it close to tell and show,

Homunculus is threshold bound,

What has been lost, will be found!

Part Four

Blessings!

*Destiny is always this very moment,
It can't be closer, it's that near,
When all is said and done my friends,
Beginnings are in their ways ends ...*

Through undergrowth of grief and sorrow,

Homunculus anticipates a new tomorrow,

A day with gleaming promise, bright,

Fleet of foot, clear of sight,

Casting off history's traumatic bane,

Cutting asunder that torturous chain,

Heaving apart a million painful barbs,

This odyssey hasn't been in vain,

A metamorphic spiral comes to rest,

With sublime peace within one's breast,

Yet today suffering must hold sway,

A funeral for every pained yesterday,

This in service of a healed future,

Whatever happens, come what may,

Sinking into great sadness weighing,

Upon a heart vulnerable, obeying,

Every shard to penetrate deeply allowing,

In humble solicitude, praying, bowing,

Homunculus is finally undergoing,

Redemption's revolution forging,

Heavy heart with pensive forbearance,

Forgoing years of sensuous gorging,

Can't all be sacrificed in a day,

Poison gradually seeping away,

Homunculus desires integrity,

Striving quietly for impeccability,

Perhaps out of reach in its totality,

Yet not a pathway of futility,

Homo-Spiritus calls from yonder,

No aim can be more fonder,

Each step a challenge to aspire,

To transcend, transform, go higher,

Beyond undergrowth, a new life,

Wilful intent, sharp as a knife!

He knows it must begin immediately,
Never is a soul somewhere other than,
The moment now, that always began,
In eternal present, living flow,
Stop, meditate and Homunculus will know,
'Tis the only time he will ever have,
From here and now, he will come and go,
Timeless time, a paradox, sacred,
An invitation to seize the present,
Isn't it for this that he was bred,
Timelessness and time mystically wed,
A vertical down flow into time,
From timeless realms he is led,

Spiritual abodes beyond time and space,

From where his soul can be fed,

Homunculus knows all this and more,

Deep inside his treasure store,

Now to aspire to loftier heights,

To raise up his eyes to greater sights,

To welcome eternity into heart and mind,

Floods of spiritually laced delights,

Discovering cosmos where it's always been,

Right here on earth, as when it did begin,

Realising why he is an embodied soul,

To integrate heaven and earth as his goal,

And within this ever present movement,

To gradually make parts into a whole,

He decides to decrease impediments now,

Acknowledging innate wisdom knows how,

For the future condition of his soul!

Final round, at least every-when,

Timeless moment comes again,

No more words beyond now and here,

All contained within this sphere,

Destiny is always this very moment,

It can't be closer, it's that near,

When all is said and done my friends,

Beginnings are in their ways ends,

And where this epic tale commenced,

In depths of spirit most entrenched,

With layers of name and form circled round,

Identity embroiled in complexity abound,

We travelled through mixed terrain,

Hearing an old, outworn refrain,

We witnessed homunculus gagged and caged,

Frustrated, anguished and enraged,

Yet where a wall, cracks appeared for sure,

Light shone through from Spirit's core,

It should be known that transformation's key,

Is in each hand for all to see,

According to a soul's capacity,

Hence with blessings from highest state,

May all who hear, take heart, instigate,

Bring homunculus into Godhead's grace,

That Homo-Spiritus can take his place,

Incarnate divine Sophia, beloved feminine,

Sacred companions entwined, embrace,

Blessings, blessings to everyone,

Who received my gift from whence it begun,

Blessings dear kith and kin, sentient creatures,

With wondrous diversity in external features,

Every bird, animal, insect, fish,

Blessings to you, peace be my wish,

And every homunculus, striving soul,

Blessings on your journey towards becoming whole,

As we all share a common bond of life,

I especially dedicate this ode to my wife!

References

1. Steiner R (2016), 'Goethe's Faust in the Light of Anthroposophy, Steiner Books, Great Barrington Massecheusets

2. Goethe JW (2005), 'Faust, Part 1', Penguin Classics, London England

www.ingramcontent.com/pod-product-compliance
Lightning Source LLC
Chambersburg PA
CBHW031427290426
44110CB00011B/554